'King of all the quarrymen' — a slate splitter, c.1880, in Cwm
Penmachno, near Betws-y-coed, Gwynedd. Photograph from the John
Thomas Collection, held at the National Library of Wales.

THE SLATE INDUSTRY

Merfyn Williams

Shire Publications Ltd

CONTENTS

Published by Shire Publications Ltd, Midland House, West Way, Botley, Oxford OX2 0PH. Copyright © 1991 by Merfyn Williams. First published 1991; transferred to digital print on demand 2011.
Shire Library 268. ISBN 978 0 74780 124 5.

Printed by PrintOnDemand-Worldwide.com, Peterborough. UK.

British Library Cataloguing in Publication Data: Williams, Merfyn. The slate industry. 1. Slate production. I. Title. 338.2757. ISBN-10: 0 7478 0124 5. ISBN-13: 978 0 74780 124 5.

Cover: A Wingrove & Rogers battery electric locomotive shunts a wagon of finished slate at Llechwedd slate quarries near Blaenau Ffestiniog on a very hot 22 June 1976. (Photograph courtesy of Kevin Lane)

ACKNOWLEDGEMENTS
The author is grateful for the help received from Dr M.J.T. Lewis, Mr R. Hefin Davies (Chairman and Managing Director, J.W. Greaves & Son), Tim and Celia Oulton, Dafydd Charles.
Illustrations are acknowledged as follows: Barrow-in-Furness Library, page 20 (bottom): *Barrow News and Mail*, page 12 (bottom): Delabole Slate Company, pages 11 (bottom), 16, 17 (bottom) and 21; Gwilyn Evans, pages 28 (bottom) and 29 (bottom); Nigel Evans, page 24 (top); J.W. Greaves & Son Ltd, pages 22 (bottom right) and 23 (bottom); Gwynedd Archives Service, pages 6 (top), 9, 11 (top), 12 (top left), 13, 15 (top), 17 (top). 18 (top and centre), 22 (top), 26 and 27 (bottom); Kendal Archives, pages 14 (top) and 27 (top); Kendal Library, page 8 (top); Cadbury Lamb, cover; McAlpines, Penrhyn Quarry, Bangor, Gwynedd, page 20 (top left); National Library of Wales, pages 1, 23 (top) and 25; Wincilate Limited Aberllefenni Slate Quarries, pages 6 (centre) and 18 (bottom). The remaining illustrations are by the author.

Slate formation. The mudstone is made up of clay minerals that realign themselves under pressure into lines parallel to the bedding called laminations. The mudstone has become shale. Further pressure and heat break down the clay minerals and they reform as different minerals such as micas along a new plane, called the cleavage, which is perpendicular to the main directions of pressure. It is along this cleavage plane that the slate splits.

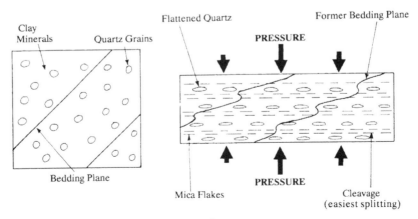

The Old Post Office at Tintagel, Cornwall, showing a mixture of slate tiles, from those of various random sizes to 'rag slate', large slates with one end left ragged, which was a Cornish practice in the eighteenth and nineteenth centuries.

THE SLATE

The word 'slate' is derived from a French verb *esclater* meaning 'to split'. This yielded the word *slat* in old English and *ysglatus* in Welsh, which in present usage has now given way to *llech*, which originally meant 'a broad, flat stone'. 'Slate' can signify a flat roof tile derived from different raw materials such as sandstone or limestone, for example the Collyweston slates of Jurassic limestone from Northamptonshire, but in this book it is confined to a particular type of rock and its products.

Slate is a metamorphic rock, that is, it has been altered from an original formation. The beginning, in most cases, is a deposition of fine sediments of clay minerals, flaky in character, forming a mudstone. The chemical composition and the nature of the deposition of the mudstone determine the eventual colour of the slate. Continual deposition over millions of years causes the flaky minerals to undergo a physical change called *dynamic metamorphism* where they reform in lines parallel to the way the rock lies — the *bedding plane*. The mudstone has now become

shale. Further pressures and great heat cause a chemical change to occur called *contact metamorphism*, where the original clay minerals break down and reform as other minerals, micas and feldspars, which become the main constituents of a new and different rock — slate. These new minerals reform along an entirely different plane from the bedding plane, called the *plane of cleavage*. It is this feature that gives the slate its splitting characteristic and hence its economic value.

Such circumstances can occur in any geological period in any part of the world, so there is, for example, Spanish slate, North African slate and Brazilian slate. However, the optimum conditions for producing the best-quality slate occurred at particular geological periods in specific areas. These areas are in Britain and are to be found in Scotland, primarily around Ballachulish, Highland; in England, in Cumbria and Cornwall; and in Wales, in north Wales and western Dyfed. Slate is still produced in Wales and England but by the second half of the twentieth century the formerly extensive industry in Scotland had become defunct.

With one exception, the rocks of all these areas belong to the Lower Palaeozoic age, that is, older than 320 million years. In Wales, the slates of the Bethesda-Nantlle Belt of northern Gwynedd belong to the Cambrian system, 500 million years old, and are of variable colour, although purple tends to dominate. The slates of the famous Ffestiniog Belt are of the Ordovician age, about 400 million years old, and are uniformly blue-grey and finer-grained than the Cambrian slates.

In Cumbria the slates are mainly Ordovician. In the Borrowdale group their original composition is of volcanic ashes called *tuffs*. This causes them to be thicker-grained and predominantly green although the colour does vary from light and dark green to purple-green. The grey and blue-black slates of the Burlington Quarries near Kirkby-in-Furness are of the Silurian age, 350 million years old.

The Delabole slate of Cornwall is younger, being of Devonian age, 345 million years old, and of variable colour from greenish grey to dark blue-grey.

The main slate belt of Scotland contained the oldest slates. They were Pre-Cambrian in origin, which means they are older than 600 million years. Very dark, almost black in colour and fine-grained, they contain

Map of slate-producing areas in the United Kingdom.

4

Stratigraphy. This diagram shows rock succession with the occurrence of slate in different geological ages in Britain. The numbers in the columns are the ages of the different geological periods in millions of years.

STRATIGRAPHY		SLATES IN WALES	OTHER SLATE AREAS
ERA	PERIOD		
CAINOZOIC	TERTIARY & RECENT 60	NO CLEAVAGE HAS BEEN DEVELOPED IN CAINOZOIC OR MESOZOIC ROCKS IN BRITAIN, BUT FISSILE ROCKS, WHICH ARE NOT TRUE SLATES, ARE FOUND IN THE JURASSIC SERIES.	
MESOZOIC	CRETACEOUS 120		
	JURASSIC 145		
	TRIASSIC 170		
PALAEOZOIC	PERMIAN 210		
	CARBONIFEROUS 280		
	DEVONIAN 320		DELABOLE (CORNWALL)
	SILURIAN 350	LLANGOLLEN, CORWEN, GLYN CEIRIOG	LAKE DISTRICT (KIRKBY)
	ORDOVICIAN 400	ABERGYNOLWYN, ABERLLEFENNI, CORRIS, LLANGYNOG FFESTINIOG DISTRICT DYFED	LAKE DISTRICT (GREEN SLATES) LAKE DISTRICT (SKIDDAW SLATE)
	CAMBRIAN 500	ARTHOG, FAIRBOURNE NANTLLE, PENRHYN, DINORWIG	
	PRE-CAMBRIAN	THE PRE-CAMBRIAN ROCKS IN WALES ARE TOO MUCH ALTERED AND CRUMPLED TO YIELD WORKABLE SLATES	CHARNWOOD FOREST (LEICESTERSHIRE) BALLACHULISH, ETC. (SCOTLAND)

impurities that tend to weather out when exposed on roofs, leaving voids in the slates.

By 1793, when the industry had begun to be placed on an organised basis, Wales was beginning to outstrip the other areas of production. Out of a total British production of 45,000 tons, Scotland produced 4000 tons, Cumbria 6000 tons, Cornwall and Devon 9000 tons, and Wales 26,000 tons.

Towards the end of the nineteenth century, when the industry reached its peak, Wales dominated production. The availability and quality of Welsh slate far outmatched the other regions in Britain. Thus in 1882, of the total tonnage of 494,100, some 451,000 (92 per cent) came from Wales, with two quarries, Penrhyn at Bethesda near Bangor and Dinorwig at Llanberis, both in Gwynedd, producing almost half of that output.

The principal use of slates is as roofing tiles, but in 1990 it accounted for only 5 per cent of the British roofing material industry. Where the plane of cleavage is not so pronounced and the rock will not split thinly, slabs are produced. These are used mainly for monumental gravestones. The best snooker tables have slate bases but these now come from Italy. Quarrymen used to make various decorative objects out of slate and this tradition is now carried on in the production of souvenirs for tourists. In the Delabole Quarry, Cornwall, in 1908 a plant was set up for crushing waste slate to dust for use as an inert material called *fullerite*, and this has also been carried out

Above: *Parc and Croesor Quarry, near Porthmadog, Gwynedd, in 1920 with 306 tonnes of slabs ready to be taken away. The different sizes give an indication of the range of uses for slate slabs, from gravestones to electricity panels.*

Right: *Fine finishing of slate at the Inigo Jones Slate Works near Caernarfon, Gwynedd. The machine at work, abrasive wheel on rotating spindle, is a rock polisher called the Jenny Lind, reputedly because the perfect finish matched the voice of the singer of that name who flourished in the second half of the nineteenth century when the machine was being developed.*

Left: *Slate fans at Llechwedd, Blaenau Ffestiniog, Gwynedd. A slate fan is purely decorative and is made by careful splitting of the slate after a hole has been drilled through the piece. The split ends are then rotated around a bolt placed in the hole. This was one of the ways quarrymen practised their skills in their spare time. The fan on the right shows that the skill has not been lost and now such work has an outlet in the tourist trade.*

Above: *A view of the Ffestiniog Slate Company Quarry, formerly Oakeley Quarry, showing the diversity of functions in late twentieth-century quarry sites. Slate extraction continues but the upper tier of buildings in the background, as well as processing slate, is the site of the Gloddfa Ganol Mountain Tourist Centre. The buildings on the lower level include, on the right, a slate mill and a plant for pulverising slate waste, which is then reconstituted with resin as moulded slate tiles, and, on the left, a carpet warehouse.*

Right: *An abandoned 'close-end', or underground quarry, in Tilberthwaite, Cumbria. Small operations such as this were found in all slate-producing regions and produced slate mainly for local use.*

at Penrhyn Quarry, Gwynedd, since the 1970s. Fullerite is used for many purposes, such as to strengthen roofing felt and submarine cables. In Ffestiniog, Gwynedd, slate waste is reduced to dust and sent in tankers to south Wales, where it is reconstituted as slate tiles. But perhaps the strangest use of all was described by F. J. North in his authoritative text *Slates of Wales*, where he quoted from the Wynn Papers (1656) of Conwy, Gwynedd: 'Hearing at Lady Anger's funeral, that he has an inward bruise caused by a fall from his horse, Robert Mostyn sends to Richard Wynn at Plas Tirion, a piece of Irish slate, to be scraped and drunk in a posset before bed time.'

Thrang Crag Slate Quarry, Great Langdale, Cumbria, in 1838. The men are using picks and bars of any sort to extract the slate blocks, which are then carried on stretchers to men close by for splitting, or riving.

EXTRACTING THE SLATE

The extraction of slate uses the same principles wherever the industry is located. These involve taking advantage of the natural weaknesses in the rock through planes and joints to take out the largest block possible from the quarry face. The larger the block, the more options become available for reduction, and the larger-sized slate tiles yield higher wages for the workers.

From the late eighteenth century explosives were used. In north Wales it is said that the quarrymen were introduced to the skill of blasting by the Cornish copper miners working at Llanberis. The type of

Right: The diagram shows the major planes in the slate vein that are used in extraction and processing. The bedding plane is the direction in which the rock lies and this is shown by the angle from the horizontal called the dip. The dip of the vein is crucial to the way it is worked. The strike is at a right angle to the bedding. The plane of cleavage is the splitting plane and perpendicular to it is the pillaring plane, along which the depth of slate blocks is obtained.

explosive used was black powder. As this was a slow-igniting powder the blast followed the natural weaknesses of the rock, thus shifting large blocks rather than shattering them. Thus the *rockmen* obtained the largest blocks for processing. In underground workings, the miners, the team of workers who *developed* the mine by opening new tunnels, used dynamite after it was discovered by Alfred Nobel in 1866.

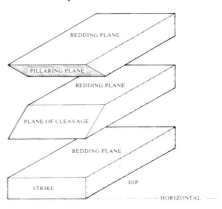

Above left: *Slate extraction at Penrhyn Quarry, near Bangor, Gwynedd, at the end of the nineteenth century. The rockmen are using the natural planes and joints in the slate to ease out the block after a blast has separated it from the quarry face. They are secured by a thick hemp rope anchored by lumps of slate on the floor above.*

Above right: *The compressed-air drill came into general use towards the end of the nineteenth century. The man is driving along the pillaring plane, as the lines in the slate behind him show. The rate of progress was improved but there was an increase in dust inhalation.*

Below: *Rockmen using a hand drill called a jumper. This had a weight at one end and the operation entailed dropping the jumper and twisting at the same time. A good rate of progress would be about 180 mm (7 inches) an hour.*

The rockmen would drill into the slate at right angles to the cleavage plane, on a direction called the *pillaring line*. In order to minimise the damage to the slate, a hand-operated tool called a *jumper* was traditionally used. Even though compressed-air drills were introduced to the slate quarries towards the end of the nineteenth century many rockmen persisted with the slower method. Hand-drilling was still in use in smaller quarries until well into the twentieth century. On completing the hole, skill was then needed to insert sufficient powder to move the rock but not to shatter it, so as to leave the maximum number of large blocks on the quarry floor.

Slate quarries can be placed in three broad categories: open, pit and underground. Where the slate was dipping steeply down a mountainside, the quarry would be developed along terraces called galleries; if the veins dipped steeply into the bottom of the valley, then the quarry would develop as a pit; in places where the slate dipped into the mountainside, extraction took place underground on floors reached by tunnels, called adits, driven from the surface.

OPEN QUARRY

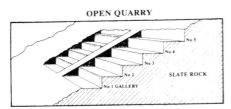

PIT QUARRY

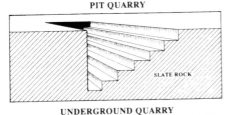

UNDERGROUND QUARRY

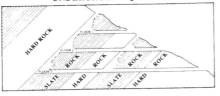

In 1948, in the Kirkby Quarry, Cumbria, another method was introduced, based on the one used in the Carrara marble quarries in Italy. This entailed driving tunnels into the rock into which a high tensile steel wire was inserted; this sliced through the slate, using a mixture of sand and water as an abrasive medium, at a rate of 2.5 to 3 cm (1 to 1¼ inches) an hour.

The major contrasts between the various extraction processes are in the way that different patterns of development progressed. These stem from the angle at which the slate veins were lying — the *dip* of the bedding plane. It was the dip of the rock that decided whether the extraction method was pit, gallery or mine.

Where the slate was dipping almost vertically into the ground this necessitated the opening of large pits. The most notable example of pit extraction is at Delabole, Cornwall, where the cavity is over 150 metres (500 feet) deep and about 1.6 km (1 mile) in circumference.

Where slate dips approximately vertically down a mountainside the open gallery method was employed. Open galleries were huge terraces ranging from 9 metres (30 feet) to 21 metres (70 feet) in depth. Galleries were first introduced by James Greenfield in 1799 at the Penrhyn Quarry, and it is there and at Dinorwig Quarry that this method is best seen.

Where the slate dipped at a more gentle angle into the mountainside it was necessary to follow the rock underground. Thus slate mines, as opposed to slate quarries, were opened. It is thought that the technique of underground extraction was initially developed in Cumbria, where this method was being followed towards the middle of the eighteenth century at Walna Scar Quarry above Seathwaite. Two men from that area, William Turner and Thomas Casson, introduced the method to north Wales when they took over a quarry in the Conwy valley in 1798 and then the Diffwys Quarry at Ffestiniog in 1799. Large cavities were carved out but in order to maintain the roofs some of the slate had to be left. Thus a system known as the *chamber and pillar* was introduced. Pillars proved to be inadequate and so a continuous line of slate

10

Penrhyn Quarry, Gwynedd, c.1870 showing the development of the gallery system. The depth of the galleries varied between 9 and 21 metres (30 and 70 feet). The column in the middle is waste rock called Y Talcen Mawr.

Delabole Quarry, Cornwall, in 1990. It is the largest pit quarry, with a depth of over 150 metres (600 feet) and a circumference of over 1.6 km (1 mile). It has been continuously worked since the late middle ages.

Left: *Llechwedd Quarry, Gwynedd, c.1880; a posed photograph. In the chamber can be seen on the left a slab wagon complete with a slab; in the middle is a finished slate wagon, empty, and on the right are men pushing a full rubbish wagon. The men with the ladder on the left are 'bad rock men'; they were employed to keep the roof of the chamber clear of loose material. The lowest man on the walkway is a steward, distinguished by the fact that he is carrying a carbide lamp rather than a candle.*

Right: *Kirkby Quarry, Furness, Cumbria, 1984. Late twentieth-century methods largely involve removing massive lumps by deep drilling and powerful explosives. This block measured 21.34 by 7.93 by 7 metres (70 by 26 by 23 feet) and weighed about 2000 tonnes.*

— a wall — had to be retained, although the term 'chamber and pillar' continued in use. In this fashion about 30 per cent of good workable slate remained in the ground. The largest slate mine in the world was at Gloddfa Ganol, Blaenau Ffestiniog, Gwynedd, which had 32 levels or floors, each about 12 metres (40 feet) deep, with about 70 km (43 miles) of connecting tunnels.

From the 1970s the practice increasingly has been to work down the pillars in the open air and very little underground operation now takes place, although it continues in the Aberllefenni Quarry in southern Gwynedd. The extraction technique has become fairly standardised. It involves using powerful explosives with huge earth-moving plant to transport great masses of material at the same time. Delabole has developed the wire-saw technique so that blocks of some 300 tonnes are sawn out at the quarry face, thus almost eliminating blasting and the accumulation of waste.

This formal photograph, probably late nineteenth-century, shows the steps involved in processing slate. After a block arrived at the working area from the workface it would be shortened by the man with the huge mallet over his shoulder. The man to his left would broadly split the block and then it would be transferred to the man smoking a pipe for fine splitting. Finally, the man in the foreground would dress the slate, that is square the sides with the knife, cutting on the fixed edge ('trafal' in Welsh).

PROCESSING THE SLATE

Slate production is a rare example of an industry where extraction of the raw material and processing to the finished product often occur on the same site.

Until the large-scale modernisation of the 1960s and 1970s the processing entailed three main stages. Firstly, a block was extracted from the quarry face and reduced at that point to a manageable size for transportation. Secondly, away from the quarry face, in a safe and clear working area, the block was reduced to a size fitting as closely as possible to the finished tile. Finally, the skilled splitter or *river* set out to obtain the maximum number of tiles and these were squared off or finished by the dresser. In Cumbria the top end of the slate was rounded off by the *whittler*. After the second stage, slate that would not split thinly would be processed into slabs.

Until the end of the eighteenth century the second and third stages were conducted in the open air and in the crudest manner. Slate tiles could be of any size or shape until standardisation was introduced in Wales by General Warburton of Penrhyn Quarry. It was he who, by 1750, had devised the scheme to name different-size slate tiles after female aristocratic titles. The largest slate was the 'queen', which could be 762 mm (30 inches) or more in length but the most popular size was the 'countess' at 508 by 254 mm (20 by 10 inches) — and these sizes are still used. Because of the coarse nature of Cumbrian slate a standard size was more difficult to achieve and so the division was between good-quality slate called 'London slate', middle quality called 'counties' and poorer material called 'tun slate' — all of random size. These Cumbrian slates were measured and sold by weight rather than by numbers as Welsh and Cornish slates were.

The Price of the Fine

LONDON SLATE,

Deliver'd on board at *Penny-bridge* in *Lancaſhire*,
Is Two Pounds One Shilling *per* Ton, neat Weight,

Freight to *Hull* about 18 *s. per* Ton.

The Ton covers about twenty-three Yards ſuperficial,
at ſevenYards to the Rood, is three Roods and
two Yards.

The Ton is 20 Hundred, the Hundred 112 Pounds.

Particulars may be had of Mr. *William Rigg*, Slate Merchant, in
Hawkſtead, Lancaſhire.

The second stage, reducing the slate into small blocks ready for splitting, consisted of two operations, broad reduction along the cleavage and cutting across (docking) the grain. This latter action was performed with a huge mallet and was carried out in the open air. As the industry became more organised, the men built shelters for themselves in the working areas to complete the third stage, the final reduction. These were three-sided structures, called *waliau* in Wales, and in some quarries they were built in rows.

Attempts were made from the outset to mechanise the processes. Mechanised timber saws were adapted to cut slate slabs, the first known example being in a mill in Rhydsarn, 2 miles (3 km) west of Blaenau Ffestiniog, in 1802. The first mills were sawing sheds that dealt primarily with slab production and were located where water power was easily available.

Buildings for housing machines were being erected from the first decade of the nineteenth century but as the techniques and power sources improved the *slate mill*

The prototype fully integrated slate mill built at Diffwys Quarry, Blaenau Ffestiniog, Gwynedd, in 1859. Blocks would enter along the right-hand wall and be reduced on the platforms; they were then transferred across to the saw tables aligned down the middle of the mill and then finished by splitting and dressing along the left-hand wall.

Llechwedd, Gwynedd, Floors 1 and 2, in the 1890s. The water is directed to the waterwheel on Floor 2 and then down to the mill at the next floor, where the tourist Slate Caverns complex is now situated.

A set of working structures called 'waliau' in a Pembrokeshire (Dyfed) Quarry in the 1920s, showing men employing the 'rhys' (wooden mallet) in the open air while the splitting and dressing is carried out under shelter.

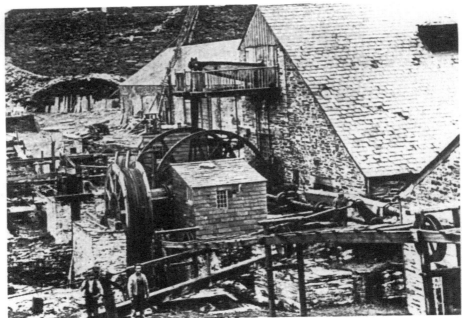

Steam engine installed at Delabole, Cornwall, in 1856. It drove two haulage drums and flat rods to a pumping engine.

was evolved. Between 1840 and 1860 more and more of the operations were brought together under one roof and powered from a single source so that a model emerged that remained essentially the same for a hundred years. Basically, this was a rectilinear building along which a main drive shaft, operated from the power source, would drive machinery such as sawing tables, planers and dressers sited in lines parallel to the drive shaft and driven from a series of intermediary shafts and pulleys.

Water power became an essential requirement in slate production as mechanisation increased. From the 1840s onwards larger concerns relied heavily on water to work the mills. However, water power was unreliable as water could be scarce in the summer and might freeze in winter. Other, more controllable sources had to be exploited although remote and lesser sites maintained their use of water. In one instance, Rhos Quarry on Moel Siabod near Capel Curig, Gwynedd, a waterwheel was

still in use when it closed in 1953.

Steam power became a more viable alternative during the nineteenth century, particularly where production warranted the expenditure. The first steam engine in the industry was a pump at Hafodlas Quarry, Dyffryn Nantlle, Gwynedd, installed in 1807 and in 1834 a steam engine called the Speedwell was installed at Delabole. It is thought that the first steam-powered mill appeared at Holland Quarry (now part of Gloddfa Ganol) in Blaenau Ffestiniog in about 1845.

It was in Blaenau Ffestiniog that innovations in mechanisation were the most effective for one important reason. The Ordovician slate was less brittle than its Cambrian counterpart and thus more amenable to machine working. The most successful innovations were made by J. W. Greaves of Llechwedd Quarry. In 1852 he invented the Greaves sawing table that replaced the more arbitrary method of the mallet in reducing slate slabs for the splitter.

A typical working area in a mill in the early part of the twentieth century, with the splitter sitting on the right. To the left, his partner is operating the Greaves rotary dresser, driven by belting from a pulley in the line shaft above.

Sand saws at Delabole. The principle was that sand would be fed under a toothless blade on the suspended carriage and would abrade the block.

Left: *The Hunter saw. This was invented in 1856 for sawing large blocks and was notable for the fact that the teeth could be removed individually for sharpening.*

Right: *Electric locomotives at work in the Croesor Quarry, Gwynedd, in 1906 — one of the earliest known sites for such an application of alternating current (AC).*

Left: *A diamond saw at work in Aberllefenni, Corris, Gwynedd, in the 1960s.*

Hitherto all attempts at mechanised dressing had been based on the guillotine or sword-arm principle but in 1856 J. W. Greaves invented a rotary machine and the version improved by his son, R. M. Greaves, in 1886 is still the one seen in slate mills throughout the world. In the same period J. W. Greaves also developed a slate-planing machine for finishing slabs.

The Greaves dressing machine was not so successful with more brittle slates and so Penrhyn Quarry continued with the treadle machine. In Cumbria, because the slates mainly consisted of coarse volcanic ash, little mechanisation took place. This is the main reason that so few buildings can be seen in the numerous disused quarries in the Lake District.

Saws were not applied to any great extent in Cumbria either but different types were used in Gwynedd and Cornwall. The universal type was Greaves's circular saw but horizontal saws were developed as well. Popular at Delabole were the sand saws as the younger Devonian slate tended to be softer than the Ordovician of Gwynedd.

During most of the nineteenth century the motive power for turning the drive shafts was either steam or water but in 1891 Llechwedd had its first electrical plant. This was replaced by a more powerful plant in 1904, still in use in 1990. In 1906 the North Wales Power and Traction Company opened its hydro-electric plant at Cwm Dyli, at the foot of Snowdon, which supplied the largest quarries in Gwynedd. Such was the demand for electricity that new power stations were opened at Maentwrog and Dolgarrog in Gwynedd in 1928.

The greater availability of power through electricity brought in new machines. In the 1930s in Gwynedd, Cumbria and Cornwall the diamond saw took over from the Greaves table. In the 1980s more sophisticated machinery was introduced where the reduction of the slate block, now coming in directly from the quarry face, is judged by computerised laser beams. Whereas previously the block had to be manhandled on to the table and manually adjusted, the whole process for the entire mill is now done by a computerised machine which needs only one operator. Mills built after the early 1980s are centred around this operation and allow much more space within the buildings for the dumper and the fork-lift truck to manoeuvre.

However, mechanisation of the splitting process has not been entirely successful and is still done largely by hand. When McAlpines took over Penrhyn Quarry in 1971 they introduced slate-splitting machines and these have also been used in Llechwedd since 1976. For the operation to be successful the quality of the slate has to be consistently good and this is not always the case. Also the slates that are mechanically split are sawn on all four edges, which means that the bevel effect of the dressing machine is lost. This has proved unpopular with customers so the technique is not widely employed.

Ynysypandy Slate Mill near Porthmadog, Gwynedd. This abbey-like structure was built in 1855 and is the sole survivor of a multi-storey slate mill. It is assumed that raw blocks entered on the upper floor and the finished product went out on the lower floor just above the fence. This is now a Guardianship Monument in the care of Snowdonia National Park.

Above left: *This man is transporting slate by sled or hurdle at Honister, Cumbria, towards the end of the nineteenth century in much the same way as travellers described the process in mountainous areas in the eighteenth century.*

Above right: *The straight lines emerging from the steep slopes of the quarry, located under the summit of the Moelwyn Mountain, Gwynedd, are inclines. These operated on the counterbalancing principle, with descending full wagons hauling empty wagons back up. In this photograph the incline disappearing into the slate waste is said to have counterbalanced a drill driving an inclined shaft.*

Below: *Part of the interior of the Burlington Quarry at Kirkby-in-Furness, Cumbria, in the 1950s. The quarry is still operational in the 1990s and stretches for 3 miles (5 km) along a ridge.*

Part of the Delabole pit, Cornwall, in the 1880s, showing at the top the headframes for haulage, called the papote head, with the chimney of a steam engine beyond. In the left foreground is the waterwheel haulage system.

TRANSPORT

The transport of slate falls into four broad categories: blocks of slate from working face to processing area; finished slate from processing area to stackyard; from stackyard to market; and the carriage and disposal of waste.

Eighteenth-century drawings show that for the first and second stages sledges were in common use. In Welsh the name for the open-sided slab wagon is *slêd*, which harks back to this origin, whilst in Cumbria it is called a *clog-bogie*. From the early nineteenth century tracks were laid, mainly of edge-rail type, and as they were crudely laid the slab wagons usually had double-flanged wheels.

As the quarries developed and mechanisation occurred processing areas became more centralised so that blocks had to be brought either up or down to them from various parts of the quarry and so the incline system was created. This was essentially a railway on a slope operated from a drumhouse. There was a wire rope which at one end would lower full wagons controlled by a brake whilst the other end would be attached to empty wagons being hauled up by the weight of the full wagons descending. For the transport of material uphill a ballast system had to be devised. It was mainly for this purpose that water balances were used. Eight vertical water-balance lifts were installed in Penrhyn Quarry in 1848.

In the pit quarries haulage was initially by hand windlasses or horse whimseys, where the load was hauled from the pit by a horse walking around a horizontal drum. At Delabole in the 1750s Thomas Avery is credited with introducing the *papote head*, the first chain-haulage system hauled by horses. The papote led to the water-powered and then steam-powered chain inclines. These were ropeways with an anchor point at the pit edge and a fixed point in the floor of the pit. Wagons were hitched to this

21

Above: *Water balances at Penrhyn Quarry, Gwynedd, late nineteenth century. Empty wagons on platforms would descend with a tank full of water beneath whilst the full wagon with an empty tank would be hauled up. In the photograph a full rubbish wagon has arrived on the floor whilst an empty one is being pushed towards the balance.*

Below left: *A Blondin re-erected at the Vivian Quarry, as part of the Welsh Slate Museum, Llanberis, Gwynedd. The Blondin was a system whereby a carriage travelled horizontally on a fixed rope and then vertically to the pit floor for hoisting. It was named after Charles Blondin, who crossed the Niagara Falls on a tightrope in 1859.*

Below right: *A transporter incline at Dinorwig Quarry, Gwynedd, about 1900. The wagons were carried horizontally on platforms, making it easier to link with different floors.*

The removal of waste always presented a problem but in this photograph it is shown how a disabled man with his horse could be put to good use. Horses were used regularly in the larger quarries until the Second World War, and in some places until the 1960s.

ropeway and hauled to the working floor. The chain inclines were in turn replaced from about 1900 by the more sophisticated, electrically driven Blondins. In this case the anchor points were on either side of the pit and the carriage could travel horizon-tally to a predetermined point and then vertically to haul up.

As at least 75 per cent of the quarried stone was unused the disposing of rubble has always been and still remains a major problem and feature of any quarry oper-

An aerial ropeway installed in 1927 to bring slate down from Honister Crag Quarry to the mill at Honister Hause, Cumbria, which closed in 1986.

This slate boat was discovered in 1988 in the mouth of the river Dwyryd, near Porthmadog, Gwynedd. It is the only known example of the river craft that brought slate from Ffestiniog to the sea from at least 1760 to 1860. It is flat-bottomed, clinker/carvel built. Carvel building was the traditional Celtic method of butting the boat's planks against each other. Clinker building, in which the planks overlap, was introduced from Scandinavia. The boat measures 7.9 metres (26 feet) from bow to stern, 2.9 metres (9 feet 6 inches) beam.

ation. In the eighteenth century a site on a ridge had the advantage that the wheelbarrows could remove the waste and let it fall down the mountainside. However, with the increase in activity, similar transport systems to those already described had to be used to remove waste. In the pit quarries of Nantlle chain inclines and powered inclines were installed to haul out the rubble. In the underground quarries Moses Kellow introduced the idea of backfilling rubble

A plate rail discovered at Diffwys Quarry, Ffestiniog, Gwynedd, in 1986, showing a well worn track of the wheel rim. A plate-rail system was laid at this quarry in 1811 and possibly in an adjoining concern later. No other quarries in Gwynedd are known to have had this type, as the others used edge rails with flanged wheels on the wagons.

into exhausted chambers in his Parc and Croesor Quarry, Gwynedd, from the 1880s.

Finished slates have been transported in a variety of ways. In Scotland men and women used to carry them on their backs in *creels*. For long distances slates were loaded into panniers on the backs of horses or mules. The most famous packhorse track is Moses' Trod, which winds its way for some 21 km (13 miles) over hill and dale from Honister Hause to the sea at Ravenglass in Cumbria. As many sites such as Honister were on steep mountainsides the first challenge was to bring the produce down to easier terrain. By around 1800 Dinorwig Quarry had an incline system to link it with the external slate carriers.

Land transport was slow and difficult so the slate carriers took the shortest route to navigable water. River and lake connections were crucial in Gwynedd and Cumbria. On the river Dwyryd, which connected the Ffestiniog slate quarries to the sea, there were six formal quays in 1833 loading slates on to around fifty small boats that would travel the 11 km (7 miles) to the sea on spring tides only.

Ships sailed from many small harbours on the west coast of Britain to destinations all over the world. In some cases, such as

24

Abereiddy in Dyfed, the slate was quarried from the cliff face and loaded directly into the ships. Porthmadog in Gwynedd became an important shipbuilding port as a result of the slate industry. Porthmadog schooners were being built until the outbreak of the First World War.

From the beginning of the nineteenth century railways began to take the trade for the home market away from the rivers and the sea. The first railway built especially for the industry was Lord Penrhyn's 60 cm (1 foot 11½ inch) gauge edge-rail route opened in 1801 from his quarry to his newly built port at Bangor. According to one account saving of power effected 'was such that ... ten horses were found sufficient to conduct a traffic which had, on a common road, required four hundred.'

Most of the narrow-gauge railways of north Wales were built to carry slate. The Ffestiniog Railway, 1836, carried the Ffestiniog slate to Porthmadog harbour; the Padarn Railway, 1843, carried slate from Dinorwig to Port Dinorwig, Y Felinheli; the Corris Railway, 1859, reached a river port on the Dyfi near Machynlleth in Powys; the Talyllyn Railway, 1865, carried slate from one quarry only, Bryneglwys at Abergynolwyn, to Tywyn and is the only line to have continued without a break in its operation.

From the 1840s the main-line railways extended their network to connect with the slate-producing regions. By 1883 Blaenau Ffestiniog had three railway companies operating from the centre of the town. The London and North Western Railway headed north through the mountain towards Llandudno Junction; the Great Western Railway went east through Bala, and the Ffestiniog went west to connect with the Cambrian Railway at Minffordd, near Porthmadog.

During the twentieth century road haulage has taken over the role of the railways and all the slate is now transported in lorries of various sizes.

The harbour at Y Felinheli (Port Dinorwig), Gwynedd, at its grandest at the end of the nineteenth century. Vessels sailed from here to such distant places as America and Australia with best Dinorwig slate.

This photograph was probably taken in the 1920s. The man in the light-coloured jacket is holding a quarryman's lunch box which held very little considering the work the men undertook.

THE PEOPLE

When the slate industry began to expand from being a predominantly local supplier of roofing tiles in the second half of the eighteenth century the best stone was found in thinly populated areas. Therefore many of the people who were influential in this formative period were newcomers and individuals of great vision and dynamism.

In 1760 Methusalem Jones had a dream where he saw beautiful slate in a remote mountain ravine. The very next day, it is said, he walked from his native Nantlle, near Caernarfon, over the harshest terrain in Snowdonia to establish the industry in Ffestiniog. Forty years later, after a short spell in Ireland, William Turner from Seathwaite, Cumbria, arrived in the same place to open a new chapter in its history. Such individuals borrowed and begged money and took on partners to get themselves established. It is no wonder that these early entrepreneurs were known as *adventurers*.

Capital came from other sources as well. The greatest influence of this period in Gwynedd was Baron Penrhyn of County Louth, who inherited the Penrhyn estate in 1782. With money from his family's sugar plantations in Jamaica he created the infrastructure for the largest of all slate quarries which still bears his family name.

These early promoters of the industry were faced with a tremendous challenge because they were taking on workers who were steeped in rural traditions and did not readily submit to organisation. Indeed, the men felt they were independent of the management.

This attitude is reflected in the manner of payment to the quarrymen. The men worked in teams and each month on *setting day* each team made a separate deal with the management on the rate of pay for the following month based on a *poundage*, a bonus for the number of slates the team anticipated it would produce within the month — the poorer the rock the higher the poundage. A team consisted of between four and six men, at least two at the quarry face extracting the rock and two men processing and finishing the slate. The team, the deal and the working place were called the *bargain*. The bargain would pay men to clear their rubble, called *rybelwyr* in Gwynedd and *rids* in Cumbria. The men had to pay for their ropes and chains, for tools and for services such as sharpening and repairing. Each week they would receive an advance of their pay, the *sub*, and if the bargain was on bad rock the men could return home at the end of the month, after the *day of the big pay*, owing money to the management. The system was open to corruption on both sides but was not finally abolished until after the Second World War, although a minimum wage clause had been in force since 1911. Other workers in the quarry, such as saw-table operators and blacksmiths, were paid by the day. Since the 1960s the practice is for the main workforce to be all on the same bonus based on production.

By its nature the work was violent. Between 1826 and 1875 there were 258 fatal accidents in Penrhyn Quarry and a Government Inquiry in 1893 found that the underground workers in the slate mines had a death rate of 3.23 per 1000, which was higher than for coal miners.

In spite of harsh and oppressive working

SLATE QUARRIES
CONISTON.

To be Let
BY TICKET,

AT THE HOUSE OF MR. DANIEL STEELE, THE BLACK BULL INN,
In Coniston, in the County of Lancaster,

On Monday, the 21st day of June, 1841,
At Four o'clock in the Afternoon,

FOR A TERM OF YEARS, AND TO BE ENTERED UPON IMMEDIATELY,

All those Extensive and Valuable

SLATE
MINES
OR QUARRIES,

Situate in the Manor of Coniston, in the said County of Lancaster ;

THE PROPERTY OF LADY LE FLEMING.

The above Quarries contain very excellent Slate, in great abundance ; persons well acquainted with Mining or Slate getting may, by skilful management, work the above Quarries to great advantage to themselves. They will be offered in such Lots as will be pointed out at the time of Letting.

Further particulars may be known by applying to THOMAS JACKSON, Esquire, of Waterhead, near Ambleside, or to Messrs. MOSER, Solicitors, Kendal.

JUNE 4th, 1841.

R. Branthwaite and Son, Printers, Kendal.

Above: *An advertisement for a sale of quarries at the Black Bull inn, Coniston, now in Cumbria, in 1841. Many quarries changed hands frequently as initially individuals, then partners and finally companies sought to make their fortunes from slate.*

Below: *A large Caban in Dinorwig Quarry, Gwynedd, in the early twentieth century. During their short lunch break the men would debate politics, discuss theology and hold cultural activities such as an eisteddfod.*

conditions within the quarries, the men developed their own institution based on the place where they ate, called, in Gwynedd, the *Caban*. This could be the crudest of structures but within it the men elected their own Chairman, Treasurer and Policeman. The Caban had strict rules of behaviour and the Policeman could impose fines for offences such as swearing and smoking at the wrong times. After lunch had been eaten, the Caban would hold a formal meeting where debates on current affairs or cultural activities such as singing and reciting would take place.

As many quarries were located high on the mountainside, many quarrymen lodged at the quarry itself in purpose-built hostels called *barracks*. For many this entailed a 30 km (20 mile) walk to reach the quarry by seven o'clock on Monday morning and to return home after the end of the morning shift on Saturday.

Above: *Y Gorlan, the chapel at Cwmorthin, a mountain valley near Blaenau Ffestiniog which had its own community life, based on its three quarries, until the Second World War.*

Below: *'Ty Uncorn' — the 'one-chimney' house. This is the last surviving example at Blaenau Ffestiniog of a method of housing where four separate homes were built around the central chimney.*

The barracks at Rhosydd Quarry, Gwynedd, nearly 457 metres (1500 feet) high on the Moelwyn Mountain. Here more than a hundred men stayed for the week in poor conditions. Despite the bleak setting and low standard of living, the men at these barracks, as at many others, held Bible classes and cultural events.

This man is demonstrating a 'car gwyllt' (wild car) in 1976. This is an example of a unique mode of man transport that operated regularly until the 1930s from one quarry at Blaenau Ffestiniog called Graig Ddu. The stout piece of wood had a small wheel in front with a brake and a bracket on the rear placed on one inner rail of the incline, whilst an iron strut balanced on the other.

Miners Bridge, Langdale, Cumbria. Quarrymen used this bridge to reach the quarries at Tilberthwaite.

In Gwynedd from the beginning of the nineteenth century settlements grew around the quarries. Living conditions in these villages were poor as they were often built on wet, poorly drained lands. The Government Inquiry of 1893 showed that the death rate for lung diseases in Britain was 3.67 per 1000 whilst the figure for Ffestiniog was 7.63 per 1000. This was mainly due to tuberculosis. The fatal effect of silicosis caused by slate inhalation was not then recognised. It was only in 1979 that the Government acknowledged it as an industrial disease meriting compensation. The focal point of the community was the chapel (nonconformist and Welsh-speaking), as shown by the fact that so many villages in the heart of Gwynedd have biblical names, such as Nebo, Cesarea and Bethesda.

In Cumbria two traditions prevailed. In the Tilberthwaite and Langdale valleys there were numerous small quarries but even at the height of their activity very few quarrymen were recorded in the censuses as many workers either lodged or also worked on farms and put their occupation down as labourers. On the other hand, at the village of Kirkby-in-Furness nearly all the men worked at the quarries and they and their dependants were called *roundheads*

Dinorwig Hospital was built in 1860 and officially opened in 1876. It provided a good service free of charge to the quarrymen and their families. Operations were carried out here until the First World War and general practice until 1940, when it became a first-aid centre. In 1979 it was opened as the visitor centre for the Padarn Country Park, Gwynedd.

after the practice of whittling the slates.

In Cornwall the village of Delabole was named after the quarry beside which it grew up and from the end of the eighteenth century the quarry supported other villages in the area, such as Port Isaac.

It is well known that miners, especially Cornishmen, were quite mobile, and so also were quarrymen. The largest movements of people amongst the slate communities were the migrations from Gwynedd to North America. In the 1840s over half of the emigrants from Wales were men from the slate districts going to open up slate quarries. In 1846 a local newspaper described the scene: 'During the last few weeks scores of quarrymen from the parishes of Llanllechid and Llanddeiniolen have emigrated to America. It was a mournful sight to witness groups of industrious, well-conducted, hard-working men winding their way seaward and bidding farewell to their native land.' These people settled in Vermont, New Hampshire and Pennsylvania and established settlements such as West Bangor, so called, it was said, because it was exactly 3000 miles (4828 km) west of Bangor in Gwynedd.

The 1840s were years of great upheaval throughout Britain as industries continued to grow apace. The quarry owners were mindful of the welfare of their workers and felt an obligation to ensure that they were of sound mind and body. From the 1840s onwards quarry hospitals and schools were established, largely at the expense of the quarry owners. Quarrymen opened benefit clubs and housing societies that were often helped by the owners. The Penrhyn Benefit Club was established by Lord Penrhyn in 1787 and then reformed in 1825 and again in 1874, when it was taken over completely by the quarrymen.

The North Wales Quarrymen's Union was established in 1874. Its fortunes fluctuated remarkably during its existence until 1922, depending on the conflicts which arose from time to time. The longest and most bitter dispute was the Penrhyn lockout, which lasted from 1900 to 1903 and became a landmark in British labour history. It was from this background that radical politicians began to emerge, the most famous being David Lloyd George.

Although the techniques of quarrying have changed considerably during the twentieth century the traditions still remain. Politics are always lively in the slate-working areas and whilst relations between workers and management are usually good disputes still occur, as evidenced by the seven-month strike in Blaenau Ffestiniog from August 1985 to March 1986.

The work is still hard but the conditions have improved significantly and good wages are being earned. The industry reached its nadir in the 1950s but since the 1970s more money has been available as the well known firms of Burlington in Cumbria, Delabole in Cornwall and Penrhyn in Gwynedd have substantial multi-national investment behind them. At the same time established businesses such as J. W. Greaves at Llechwedd, Ffestiniog, and Wincilate at Aberllefenni, Corris, continue to thrive and new companies such as Nationwide Slate Products have entered the business.

Towards the end of the twentieth century the future looks promising for the continued use of the beautiful slate of Cumbria, Cornwall and Gwynedd.

Burlington: the name is almost synonymous with south Lakeland slate. Some quarries are still fully operational, which sometimes brings conflict with the Lake District National Park.

FURTHER READING

There is no book readily available that describes the industry in Britain as a whole. Some accounts were written in the nineteenth century and there are papers in specialised journals that are now out of print or difficult to get hold of. The places to visit listed below have excellent publications, too numerous to list here, relating mainly to their particular concerns.

Jones, R. Merfyn. *The North Wales Quarryman*. University of Wales, 1981.
Lewis, M. J. T. *Llechi: Slate*. Gwynedd Archives Service, 1976.
Lewis, M. J. T. *Sails on the Dwyryd*. Snowdonia National Park Study Centre, 1987.
Lewis, M. J. T., and Williams, M. C. *Pioneers of Ffestiniog Slate*. Snowdonia National Park Study Centre, 1987.
Lindsay, Jean. *A History of the North Wales Slate Industry*. David and Charles, 1974.
Postlethwaite, J. *Mines and Mining in the English Lake District*. First edition 1887; reprinted in facsimile, Michael Moon, 1987.

PLACES TO VISIT

There are hundreds of abandoned slate mines and quarries in highland Britain. These sites are privately owned and potentially dangerous. Do not visit without having first obtained permission from the owner. Private exploration is not necessary as the slate industry is well served with museums and exhibition quarries are open to the public. These are listed below. Intending visitors are advised to find out the opening times before making a special journey.

Carnglaze Slate Caverns, St Neot, Liskeard, Cornwall. Telephone: 01579 320251.
Chwarel Hen Llanfair Slate Caverns, Llanfair, Harlech, Gwynedd.
  Telephone: 01766 780247.
Delabole Slate Quarry, Pengelly, Delabole, Cornwall. Telephone: 01840 212242.
Gloddfa Ganol Slate Mine, Blaenau Ffestiniog, Gwynedd LL41 3NB.
  Telephone: 01766 830664.
Inigo Jones Tudor Slate Works, Y Groeslon, Caernarfon, Gwynedd LL54 7UE.
  Telephone: 01286 830242.
Llechwedd Slate Caverns, Blaenau Ffestiniog, Gwynedd LL41 3NB.
  Telephone: 01766 830306. Website: www.llechwedd-slate-caverns.co.uk
National Slate Museum (National Museums Wales), Gilfach Ddu, Llanberis, Caernarfon,
  Gwynedd LL55 4TY. Telephone: 01286 870630. Website: www.museumswales.ac.uk
North Cornwall Museum and Gallery, The Clease, Camelford, Cornwall PL32 9PL.
  Telephone: 01840 212954.

Below: Groes y Afon Quarry located 381 metres (1250 feet) above sea-level on the moors above Blaenau Ffestiniog. Reopened in 1988 near a site first worked in 1802, it is now operated by Nationwide Slate Products.